Supporting Children with

Speech and Language Difficulties

Hull Learning Services

  **David Fulton** Publishers

David Fulton Publishers Ltd
The Chiswick Centre, 414 Chiswick High Road, London W4 5TF

www.fultonpublishers.co.uk

David Fulton Publishers is a division of Granada Learning, part of ITV plc.

First published in Great Britain by Hull Learning Services.

Note: The right of the authors to be identified as the authors of this work has been asserted by them in accordance with the Copyright, Designs and Patents Act 1988.

Copyright © David Fulton Publishers 2004

British Library Cataloguing in Publication Data
A catalogue record for this book is available from the British Library.

ISBN 1 84312 225 1

Typeset by Matrix Creative, Wokingham
Printed and bound in Great Britain

Contents

iii

Foreword

This book was written in partnership with Kingston Upon Hull Special Educational Needs Support Service (SENSS) and the Hull and East Riding Speech and Language Therapy Support Service.

It is one of a series of eleven titles, providing an up-to-date overview of special educational needs for SENCOs, teachers and other professionals and parents. It was produced in response to the needs of a growing number of children requiring support with speech and language difficulties.

It has been written and compiled by:

Cathy Allenby and Judith Fearon-Wilson
(Kingston Upon Hull SEN Support Service).

Thanks are given to the Hull and East Riding Speech and Language Therapy Support Service for their guidance when compiling this book.

Our thanks too to senior adviser John Hill for his support and encouragement throughout the development of this series.

For details of other titles and how to order, please see page 70.

Introduction

(taken from 'I CAN', the national educational charity for children with speech and language difficulties)

For most children, learning to communicate is something that happens naturally. However, for some children, something goes wrong. It's not always known why it happens, but it's more common than most people think. It has been estimated that over one million children in the UK have some kind of speech and language difficulty, which is equivalent to around one child in every classroom.

What is a speech, language or communication difficulty?

The term 'speech, language and/or communication difficulty' is an umbrella term, covering a wide range of speech, language and communication delays and disorders,

- Some children may have difficulty using certain sounds in words and can be unintelligible when they talk.
- Others have difficulty understanding words. Their vocabulary is small and they find gaining and remembering words extremely hard. These children need a lot of help extending their vocabulary, for example in school with subjects such as history and science, which have many specialist words.
- Some children have severe problems with grammar. For example, they might not be aware of the 'ed' marker at the end of a regular verb. As a result they would describe something that happened in the past as in the present tense.
- Others have difficulty coping with the order of words. A sentence such as 'the boy was pushed by the girl' may be interpreted as 'the girl was pushed by the boy'.
- Some children have none of the above difficulties. They can pronounce words clearly, learn and remember new words and are able to put them in the right order using the correct grammar. Their difficulty lies in understanding or using words which express abstract ideas. Concepts such as time and distance hold little or no meaning. Their language is at a very literal level and they often do not see hidden meanings or implications.
- Language difficulties can affect children's ability to read and write. For example, if children are not perceiving sounds accurately they won't be able to reproduce them in spoken or written form.
- We use language to form relationships with others. Some youngsters with language difficulties find building friendships very difficult.

This is only a selection of the language and communication difficulties that children may experience and many may be affected by more than one.

Speech difficulties are easy to spot. By contrast, language difficulties can be more difficult to pinpoint and diagnose. In fact the latter are often called the 'hidden' learning difficulty. It is vital that class teachers feel that they are able to identify difficulties and incorporate appropriate objectives and strategies into their planning and differentiation.

The aim of this book is to provide class teachers with suggestions that will help them feel more able to support these children in school.

Inclusion in education

The concept of inclusion is enshrined within the SEN and Disability Act 2001.

Implications of the Disability Discrimination Act (1995) as amended by the SEN and Disability Act 2001

Part one of the Act:

- strengthens the right of children to be educated in mainstream schools;
- requires LEAs to arrange for parents and/or children with SEN to be provided with advice on SEN matters, and also a means of settling disputes with schools and LEAs (parent partnership services and mediation schemes);
- requires schools to tell parents where they are making special educational provision for their child and allows schools to request a statutory assessment of a pupil's needs.

In accordance with the above Act:

LEAs and schools must:

- not treat disabled pupils less favourably;
- make reasonable adjustments so that the physical, sensory and learning needs of disabled pupils are accommodated, in order that they are not put at a substantial disadvantage to pupils who are not disabled. The Disability Rights Code of Practice for schools will provide advice on what is or is not reasonable in terms of adjustments and on matters relating to admissions to schools and inclusion in school activities;
- plan strategically and make progress not only in increasing physical accessibility to the schools' premises and to the curriculum, but also in improving the delivery of written information in an accessible way to disabled pupils (i.e. access to the curriculum via oral means, as well as the written word).

Definition of disability

- The Disability Discrimination Act uses a very broad definition of 'disability'. A person has a disability if he or she has a physical or mental impairment that has a substantial and long-term adverse effect on his or her ability to carry out normal day-to-day activities.
- The DDA definition of disability covers physical disabilities, sensory impairments, such as those affecting sight or hearing, and learning difficulties.

In order to understand the issues of **speech**, **language** and **communication** difficulties within the framework of the inclusion agenda, the following statements should be taken into consideration:

- Inclusion recognises that all children have different abilities and experiences and seeks to value and gain from these differences. It is not about expecting or trying to make everyone the same or behave in the same way.
- Inclusion in education involves the process of increasing the participation of students in, and reducing their exclusion from, the cultures, curricula and communities of local schools.
- Inclusion involves restructuring the cultures, policies and practices in schools so that they respond to the diversity of students in their locality.
- Inclusion is concerned with the learning and participation of all students vulnerable to exclusionary pressures, not only those with impairments or those who are categorised as having 'special educational needs'.
- Inclusion is concerned with improving schools for staff as well as for students.
- A concern with overcoming barriers to the access and participation of particular students may reveal gaps in the attempts of a school to respond to diversity more generally.
- All students have a right to an education in their locality.
- Diversity is not viewed as a problem to overcome, but as a rich resource to support the learning of all.
- Inclusion is concerned with fostering mutually sustaining relationships between schools and communities.
- Inclusion in education is one aspect of inclusion in society.

An inclusive culture is one in which:
- Everyone is made to feel welcome.
- Students help each other.
- Staff collaborate with each other.
- Staff and students treat one another with respect.
- There is a partnership between staff and parents/carers.
- All local communities are involved with the school.
- Staff and governors work well together.

Inclusive values are established when:
- There are high expectations of all students.
- Everyone has a philosophy of inclusion.
- Students are equally valued.
- Staff seek to remove all barriers to learning and participation in school.
- The school strives to minimise discriminatory practices.

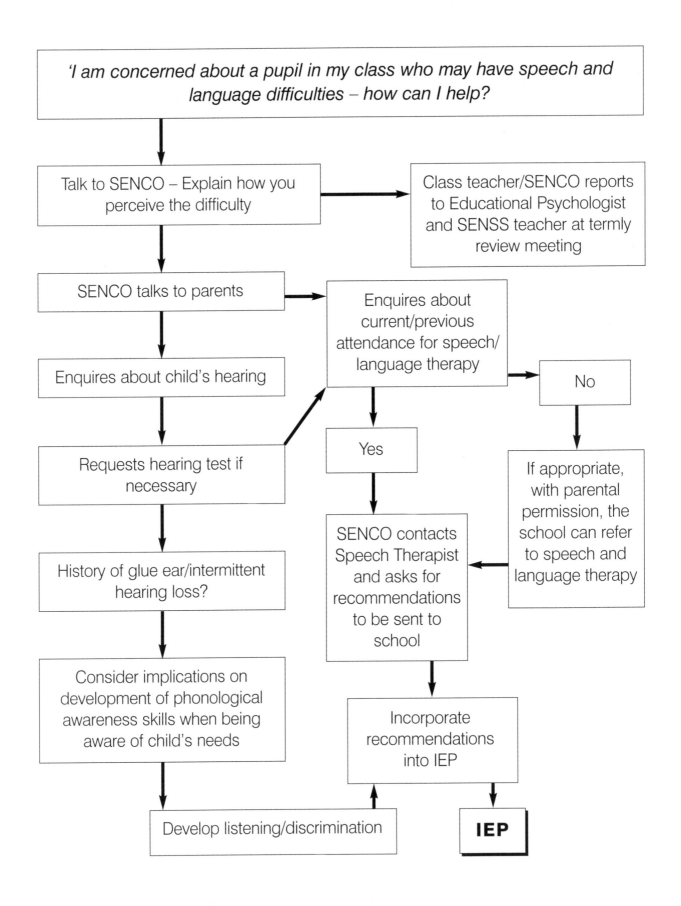

'I am concerned about a pupil in my class who may have speech and language difficulties – how can I help?

Talk to SENCO – Explain how you perceive the difficulty

Class teacher/SENCO reports to Educational Psychologist and SENSS teacher at termly review meeting

SENCO talks to parents

Enquires about current/previous attendance for speech/language therapy

Enquires about child's hearing

No

Requests hearing test if necessary

Yes

If appropriate, with parental permission, the school can refer to speech and language therapy

History of glue ear/intermittent hearing loss?

SENCO contacts Speech Therapist and asks for recommendations to be sent to school

Consider implications on development of phonological awareness skills when being aware of child's needs

Incorporate recommendations into IEP

Develop listening/discrimination

IEP

Attention, listening and memory skills

The following pages look at the areas of attention control, listening skills, memory and phonological awareness, which, while not language skills in themselves, are all vital precursors to language and learning.

Attention control refers to the ability to focus on a task and switch attention between activities. A school-age child would be expected to listen to information from the teacher while engaging in an activity at the same time. A child who is unable to do this will be at a considerable disadvantage. Language learning requires a fairly mature level of attention control.

Similarly if *listening skills* are poor, the child will find it difficult to learn new vocabulary and to acquire more sophisticated language skills. S/he may have difficulty developing the phonic skills necessary to be an effective reader.

The role of short-term *auditory memory* is also of great importance for it allows the child to hold and process information. The child who has memory difficulties will be unable to respond to follow instructions within the classroom and may well go on to have difficulties with reading.

Phonological awareness is the ability to recognise sounds within words. This may include recognising and discriminating between sounds within words, hearing and providing rhyming words or breaking up words into syllables. All these skills are important in the development of both spoken and written language.

Attention control – developmental stages

(Helping Language Development, from Cooper, Moodley and Reynell)
(Age levels are approximate; there is great variability.)

Stage I During first year of life

Extreme distractibility – child's attention held momentarily by whatever is the dominant stimulus.

Stage 2 Second year

Inflexible and rigid attention – child can concentrate for some time on a task of his/her own choice, but cannot tolerate any adult intervention. Attention level is best where the activity is one of his/her own choosing.

Stage 3 Third year

Single-channelled attention, but becoming more flexible. With adult's help can focus attention. Child can transfer from his task to adult's direction, and back to task. Attention is still adult directed making it necessary for the teacher to ensure s/he has the child's attention before giving instructions.

Stage 4 Fourth year

Still single-channelled to one task, but child can now transfer it spontaneously. Moves gradually to the stage where s/he only needs to look at the speaker if directions are difficult to understand.

Stage 5

Two-channelled attention, where the child is now able to attend to verbal instructions in relation to the task without actually looking at the adult. Attention can only be sustained for short periods for time.

Stage 6

Mature school entry level, where integrated attention is well established and well sustained.

N.B. May see fluctuating levels depending on environment or task complexity.

General activities and strategies to develop attention and listening skills

- Work with the child in a quiet, distraction-free environment, thus allowing the child to focus on the activity presented.

- Gradually start to work with the child in their normal environment as this allows his/her gradually to accommodate the distractions normally present and begin to focus on the activity.

- Ensure that the activities are both interesting and developmentally appropriate for the child.

- To engage the child's interest, always address him/her by name and when s/he has responded, encourage eye contact with the speaker.

- Try to establish shared attention to a common point of reference where possible.

- Encourage the child to follow your line of gaze or notice as you point to things, for example, looking at books and exploring objects and activities together will encourage a common shared interest.

- Accompany verbal requests to 'look' by clearly pointing to the item.

- Make the most of any opportunity to give the child guidance in order to proceed with, or complete, an activity. Do not always allow a free hand to complete tasks. Instead you can build in adult direction, for example, by spreading out the pieces of a jigsaw puzzle and indicating, by pointing to the piece you want them to select, and saying, 'where does this piece go?'

- Be sure to give praise when the child responds appropriately.

- Use simple construction or pull-apart toys to demonstrate, 'which piece goes where?'

- Choose activities which are easy to complete so that your guidance is needed. Use language models such as, 'look', it goes here' or 'this piece now'.

- The child will benefit from 'copy cat' games, where they have to copy actions modelled by the adult. Encourage them to copy your actions, which should always be accompanied by spoken instructions, for example, 'clap your hands, tap your feet', etc.

- Encourage the child to join in with finger rhymes and action rhymes.

- Note when the child is more likely to use eye contact spontaneously. Reinforce this by repeating these activities whenever possible.

- Keep language clear and simple. Try to ensure that the child gives you his full attention by saying, 'Peter, look at me and listen.'

- The child will need to play games that develop turn-taking skills. Interactive stories and lift-the-flap books can be used where the child will take turns to lift the flaps, etc. Taking turns to play a musical instrument will also help to develop turn-taking skills.

For many children, these activities begin on a 1:1 basis before moving to a small group setting. It is important that when working in a small group you consider the attention levels of the other children so that you can differentiate the activity appropriately.

Specific strategies to develop Attention Levels 1–5

Level 1

Aim To attract and sustain the child's attention to people, objects and events in his/her environment.

- Encourage good eye contact by drawing attention to your eyes and saying 'Can you look at my eyes?' – anything to get the child looking at your face.
- Use the child's name frequently, but make it purposeful.
- Visual prompts and signs can also be used to sustain attention and understanding.

Level 2

Aim To help the child tolerate the adult's presence and involvement in an activity.

- First sit with him/her and watch.
- Then sit beside him/her and engage in parallel play.
- When the child can tolerate the adult and begins to imitate the adult, small modifications can be made to his/her own play, e.g. pass a jigsaw piece to him/her or add a brick.
- Gradually accompany actions with integral verbal instructions, e.g. 'The brick goes on top.'

Level 3

Aim To establish the child's own control over his/her focus of attention. Some of these activities are suitable for a small group.

- Present the child with task materials and allow a few minutes for exploratory play. Before giving any verbal directions make sure that s/he is sitting still and is not fiddling with the toys then call his/her name, establish eye contact and deliver a short simple instruction, e.g. ask the child to copy shapes onto paper.
- The next step is to gain the child's attention while s/he is actively engaged in the task. Call his/her name, say 'look', 'listen', but do not give an instruction until you have established eye contact.
- Gradually decrease the number of alerting activities needed, until the child can look up and listen when just his/her name is called.

Level 4

Aim To begin to transfer attention skills to the group or classroom. Slowly teach the child to listen and take in what you say without stopping what s/he is doing, by following these steps:

- Alert the child to your presence while s/he is performing a task, e.g. jigsaw, by calling his/her name and giving a brief clear instruction.
- Stand by the child without speaking until s/he is aware of you, and then give the instruction.
- If the child looks up at you encourage him/her to continue with the task with comments such as 'don't look up, that's very good.'
- Stand behind the child occasionally, while commenting on his/her activity. S/he cannot therefore look at you without turning right around.

Level 5

Aim To increase the child's concentration span and continue to transfer to the classroom situation.

- The child should now be able to work alongside another child doing the same activity.
- Increase his/her tolerance by including him/her in a small group of children with a similar attention level.

Language and listening

If listening skills are poor, the child will find it difficult to learn new vocabulary and to acquire more sophisticated language skills. S/he may also have difficulty developing the phonic skills necessary to be an effective reader.

Necessary skills required for reading include:

1. **Perceptual maturity** to recognise printed shapes (2.6 to 3.6 years).

2. **Ability to recognise sound units**
   - Pre-school ability to detect rhyme and alliteration is a good indicator of reading success (Bradley & Bryant 1985).
   - Children who have difficulty analysing sounds at age 6 are likely to be reading and spelling poorly at age 9.
   - The Bradley and Bryant study of 400 children found that 'rhyme' tests were easier than initial sound tests for 4- and 5-year-olds. They felt this was because the children had experienced rhyme at pre-school, as part of songs and chants.
   - Fox and Routh (1976) showed that it is possible to teach 4-year-olds to blend (c-a-t).
   - Treiman (1985) found that children aged 4.5 to 6 years find it hard to identify the individual consonants in consonant blends.

3. **Good vocabulary and ability to use and understand spoken language.**

4. **A wide range of experiences** – vital to expand language experiences.

5. **An interest in books.**

6. **Ability to concentrate.**

Processing information in the class

(based on Ellis and Young model in reading)

Weaknesses at any stage can affect the later processes. Strengths can be used to support weaker processes.

Auditory processing

- Identifies individual sounds from speech.
- Copes with background noise and mispronunciations.
- Poor skills affect the development of the semantic system.

Visual processing

- Important features are recognised and matched to a store of known words.

The semantic system

- A store for word meanings and associations.
- Word-finding difficulties can be seen if the semantic fields are weak, e.g. lion/tiger, plum/pear.
- The system may be weak because of poor auditory processing but can also support auditory discrimination difficulties.

Letter–sound conversion

- Letters are converted into speech sounds.

Assembly

- The spoken word is stored and accessed here.
- There can be errors such as 'par cark'.
- Words do not have to be spoken aloud. They can be read using the 'inner voice'.

How does a child process language?

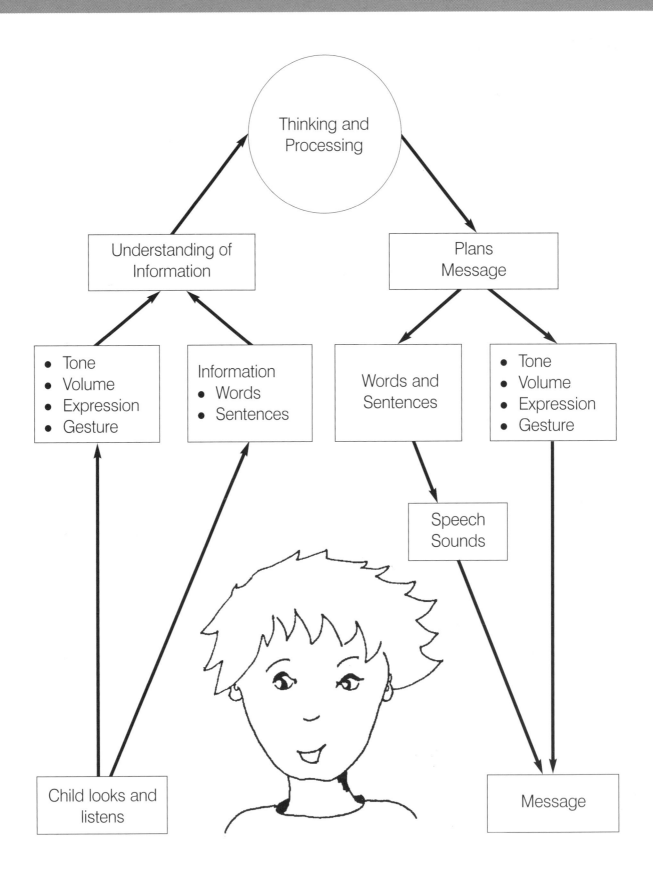

Thinking and Processing

Understanding of Information

Plans Message

- Tone
- Volume
- Expression
- Gesture

Information
- Words
- Sentences

Words and Sentences

- Tone
- Volume
- Expression
- Gesture

Speech Sounds

Child looks and listens

Message

Listening skills

Why do children have difficulty listening?

Previous experiences of listening may not match school expectations

- Language at home is usually conversational, with each person contributing in turn to the interaction.

- Language at school is less about the 'here and now' and more about the 'past and future'.

- Language in school becomes more formalised, e.g. discussions and debates. In school, children are expected to follow stories or factual accounts or perhaps make sense of directions or instructions. These are familiar classroom activities which require more sophisticated skills than simply following a conversation.

- In school, language is no longer presented as a conversation. The children may be required to listen for longer periods of time than they would usually.

- Much of the language used at home is to do with what the child has experienced or is about familiar events and people.

- Language heard at home may be supported by visual material (e.g. television). This enables the listener to pick up on information s/he has not necessarily heard or understood.

There may be physical or neurological difficulties

- The child may have had hearing problems including 'glue ear'.

- Difficulties picking out relevant signals from background noise.

- Auditory processing difficulties which may make it difficult to perceive and produce.

- Extended listening requires practice and usually requires a response.

Understanding

- Specific difficulties with understanding and using the rules of language.

- Some children are unable to cope with understanding too much information. As a result they may switch off and not listen well, but the root of the difficulty lies in understanding.

Motivation

- Anxiety and stress may make a child withdrawn and unable to participate.

- ADHD – Attention Deficit Hyperactivity Disorder.

- Children can either be ready and eager to listen or they may be switched off and unwilling to listen for other reasons.

Promoting listening skills required for the school environment

Pupils need to learn how to become active thinkers in school situations and to cope with more complex language such as prediction and hypothesis.

As mentioned above, many young children experience difficulties trying to keep up with the pace of learning currently required by the Literacy Strategy. It is vital therefore that they are taught the skills required for good listening and are able to think clearly and formulate their own ideas.

Helping children with listening difficulties

- Check the child's hearing.
- Check whether the child understands.
- Practise 'active listening' (see below).
- Practise listening in simple games and activities (see suggestions).
- Monitor listening skills throughout activities.
- Discuss the consequences of correct and incorrect behaviours within an activity.
- Encourage evaluation of others' listening skills.
- Encourage evaluation of child's own listening skills.

Teaching 'active listening'

Some children need to learn about listening by talking about it and practising it in simple activities.

What does listening involve?
Identify the associated behaviours to do with listening:

- Looking at the person.
- Concentrating on a shared topic.
- Being still.

'Active listening' involves the use of simple strategies that encourage the listener to participate actively in the learning environment. This may involve asking for clarification if understanding breaks down.

The child will need to be taught the rules for 'good listening' and to be helped to recognise these behaviours in him/herself and others. Role play will be useful to demonstrate '**good** listening' and '**not good** listening'. This can be carried out in a group situation.

The rules are:

- Sitting still.
- Looking at the speaker.
- Thinking about the words.

See the **'Good Listening Rules'** chart in the Appendix.

So, while the teacher speaks, another adult could deliberately fidget, stare out of the window, or answer incorrectly, so that the children can call out 'not sitting still!' or 'not looking!' or 'not thinking!' as appropriate. When the children recognise these behaviours in others it will be possible to tell them in a completely neutral voice that they are not doing 'good sitting', etc.

Pupils need to realise that they have to be ready to listen. Attention to how they sit and where they look is one of the first steps and precedes the thinking part of the activity. Once the children appear focused they need to take part in a range of activities that promote thinking skills.

It is also important to praise the behaviour of the children in the group and give them clear feedback. This will provide good role models for the child.

It is important to be interactive with the child to make learning happen.

Transfer to classroom – we cannot expect children to do it immediately in the classroom. Encourage transfer of skills gradually.

Introduce activities which require a response:

- ✔ Oral comprehension tasks.
- ✔ Auditory odd-one-out activities.
- ✔ Word association games.
- ✔ Following instructions.

Monitor the responses

- If someone cannot provide an appropriate response, come back to them on another occasion. Some children think that once they have had their turn they can sit back passively.
- Analyse incorrect responses and try to work out why the child made the error, e.g. was s/he not listening or was some part of the question or subject matter not understood?
- Are there particular types of activity which are proving difficult? Consider why this may be so.

Activities to improve listening ability

- **Read the child a story** – ask him/her to signal to you whenever s/he hears a particular word, e.g. an animal noise or a child's name.

- **Listen to different sounds/noises** – ask the child to signal only when s/he hears a particular sound.

- **Sequence different sounds in the correct order** – ask the child to identify various sounds and then make two sounds and ask him/her to recall the order in which they were made. Then try three, four sounds.

- **Ask the child to listen in a quiet environment** and then ask him/her to draw the things s/he hears.

- **Listen for your sound game** – make up a story that requires each child in the group to respond with a sound every time the child hears the name of the object/animal, e.g. doorbell, telephone, radio, cat. As the story will be made up by the teacher/adult the responses from the pupils can direct the listening responses required.

- **Where is the sound coming from?** – ask the child to stand in the centre of a circle with his/her eyes closed. Somebody from the circle makes a noise, e.g. clapping, and the child has to identify where the sound is coming from.

- **Hide a clockwork toy** somewhere in the room. Ask the child to find it by listening. Gradually make the sounds quieter.

- **Listen for loud and soft sounds** – use a variety of items to help the child discriminate the differences.

- **Make up silly sentences** – look at a picture together and make some deliberate, silly mistakes when talking about it. Encourage the child to tell you what is wrong.

- **Instructional activities** – colouring/drawing pictures from precise details, e.g. draw a house shape, put four windows on it, draw a tree, put apples on it, etc. Make it into a game by using an 'alarm', e.g. a shaker or drum. If the child does something wrong sound the 'alarm'. Each time the alarm goes off s/he loses a life.

- **'Simon Says', 'Musical Statues'** – a variation on Musical Statues is when the music stops, ask the pupils to do something, e.g. clap hands, touch nose, sit down.

All games need to be cognitively simple. This is important to keep the emphasis on developing listening.

Listening and auditory memory

Memory skills play an important part in understanding and using language effectively. A child's difficulties in following instructions may, to varying degrees, be due to problems of auditory short-term memory.

For example, if the class teacher says to a class, 'Finish the sentence you are on, put away your pencils, close your books and line up at the door', there are some children for whom this will represent a memory-overload. If these children also have difficulties with the syntax and grammar involved, then their difficulties will be compounded.

Strategies to aid auditory memory skills

Multi-sensory strategies

✔ **Touch** (holding an object or simply touching it)

✔ **Visualising** (looking at the object or picturing it in your mind)

✔ **Verbalising** (repeating what it is you wish to remember)

(These skills are hierarchical and as the child develops s/he will be able to call on each of these areas to a greater degree.)

✔ **Put spoken language into separate units of meaning.** Speak clearly and pause between each part of the instruction/explanation, e.g. 'Put your book in the tray/give your pencil to Peter/and read a book'.

✔ **Ask the child to repeat the message or instruction** to ensure that s/he has understood. This will check if the child has grasped the main points.

✔ **Use visual reminders** in the form of objects, pictures, simple drawings or symbols in a simple checklist (see visual memory recommendations).

✔ **Encourage the child to seek clarification.** If the child forgets encourage him/her to ask for clarification. It is important that the adult models exactly what the child needs to say, e.g. 'Can't remember the last bit, can you say it again please?' etc. Praise other children in the class when they seek clarification so that it is seen as a sensible strategy when the child is unsure.

Strategies to aid auditory memory skills...cont'd

✔ **Barrier games** – the teacher and child sit with a screen between them. The teacher provides the child with a piece of paper and gives the child simple drawing/colouring instructions. The teacher also draws/colours the precise instructions s/he gives the child. When the barrier is removed the child has instant feedback.

✔ **Sing songs and rhymes to build auditory memory.**
e.g.

a) 'I went to the shop and I bought...' game. The first child says an item then the next child says the first item and another and so on.

b) 'I packed my case and I took...' game.

c) 'I went to the zoo and I saw...' game.

At a slightly higher level:

d) 'I went to the library and I read...'

e) 'I went to the cinema and I saw...'

✔ **Read stories in small groups.** Gradually lengthen them. Ask the pupils to recall in a simple sequence. (Simple repetitive stories that are interactive can be used at first.)

✔ **Use both taped stories and dramatised stories.**

✔ **Develop auditory sequencing by encouraging the pupils to select objects at a fast pace.**

✔ **Teach the child the language of sequencing: first, next, last, start, finish, etc.**

✔ **Use 'circle time' activities** (see recommendations in section on 'Circle Time'). Pass an object around a circle and everybody makes a comment about it. No repetitions are allowed, e.g. 'It is yellow', 'It is for eating', 'It tastes sour', etc.

Phonological awareness

Phonological awareness and literacy development

Phonological awareness is the ability to perceive sounds within words.

It can also be defined as the development of sound skills that precedes literacy development.

Research has shown that *delayed development of phonological awareness skills can manifest itself initially in speech development difficulties and later in the development of early literacy skills* (Bradley & Bryant 1983).

Findings consistently confirm that of all the factors that can predict a child's later reading success (e.g. intelligence, being read to, language ability) the most powerful is the level of phonological awareness possessed by the child in the first year at school.

Research also tells us that phonological awareness can be taught and that to be most effective in literacy development, once the prerequisite sound skills have been taught, the programme should formally introduce the link between sounds and letters.

Phonological awareness skills include:

- Rhyming — of words ending with the same group of sounds
- Alliteration — of beginning sounds
- Isolation — of sounds within words, e.g. initial sounds
- Segmentation — of sentences and words into component parts
- Blending — of word parts and sounds into words
- Exchange — of sounds to make new combinations, e.g. mat–pat

---

Teaching phonological awareness

Many phonological awareness training programmes have been developed and are available from various sources. While they differ in presentation and in the resources provided, there is an overall pattern in the stages of development and order of activities prescribed; they include:

Stage 1	***Listening to sounds***	
Rhyming	–	recognition, matching, odd-one-out activities
Alliteration	–	beginning sounds
Stage 2	***Awareness of rhyme***	
Rhyming	–	creation of rhyme *e.g. Which one sounds the same as ...?* *Tell me a word that rhymes with ...?*
Alliteration	–	beginning sounds *e.g. Which one starts the same as ...?*
Isolation	–	beginning and ending sounds *e.g. What is the last sound you hear in ...?*
Segmentation	–	syllables, 2- and 3- phoneme words *e.g. How many beats/syllables can you hear in ...*
Stage 3	***Using skills to manipulate other sounds/words***	
Segmentation	–	identification of sounds/phonemes in 3- and 4-letter words *e.g. /c/a/t/, /h/e/n/*
Blending	–	3- and 4-phoneme words, blending together to make words *e.g. c-a-t*
Exchanging	–	substitution, deletion, recognising patterns in words *e.g. cap, map, tap*

Develop an awareness of **rhyme** and **rhythm (syllables)**

- Which two rhyme? cat/hat/dog.
- Child provides rhyming word with cat/dog/tree (including nonsense words).
- Play rhyme riddles, e.g. 'Mr Paul is very...'
- Listen and count beats in music; link this to the way we speak in rhythm.
- Clap out rhythm in a word phrase, e.g. el/e/phant, bread, but/ter (i.e. syllables).

Develop an awareness of **initial letter sounds**

- Teach how the sounds of words are formed in the mouth.
- Teach first, exaggerated sounds: **f/m s/l n/r v/z**.
- Ensure that children are taught to listen to the close differences in sounds

  e.g. **p/b**   unvoiced/voiced
  t/d   "   "
  k/c/g   "   "
  s/z   "   "
  f/v   "   "
  m/n   fine discrimination of sound.

- Ensure that initial sounds are not combined with 'u' to sound like 'muh', 'luh', 'suh' as this may only hinder development of good blending skills.
- Play 'Granny went to market...' – buy something beginning with same letter.
- Give pictures to sort according to initial letter sound.
- Tongue-twisters using initial letter sounds and extend alliteration skills, e.g. 'Sammy seal saw a seagull.'
- Invent a monster that eats things beginning with '**m**' – 'Can he eat a cat, jam?' etc.
- Choose any word (e.g. from NLS text) and ask children to listen and say what sound they hear at the beginning of the word.
- Use alliteration (i.e. same sound) to help children remember short vowel sounds, e.g. 'a' apple; 'e' egg.
- Say a word, e.g. 'jam' and then say it omitting the final consonant – 'ja_' and ask children to say which letter/sound is missing.

Onset/rime skills and blending skills

Develop an awareness of the *initial, final & medial* sound in cvc words

- Play game with cvc picture word cards, e.g. pan, web, cat, etc. Take turns to pick up card and ask the children to listen and identify the position of **initial, final** and **medial** sound. Give all children the chance to role reverse and play the teacher – this helps to develop confidence. Develop identification of the position of sounds in words until the children are fully confident in sound discrimination.

Develop an awareness of onset and *rime*

- Write the five vowels on the whiteboard in a column.

- Add a consonant after the vowel, e.g. **at, et, it, ot, ut**. Play lots of games ensuring that the children have grasped sound/symbol relationship. Continue with other consonants aiming for blending fluency.

- Write onsets on the board and ask the children to blend them with the rime 'at', e.g. b**at,** h**at,** s**at,** m**at,** etc. Nonsense words help to develop accuracy in blending. Divide onset/rime in only one place: b/**at**.

- It is very important to develop fluency in blending so that children can hear the letters blend together.

- When a child can read any word with an obvious rime pattern, teach other words that follow the pattern, e.g. sight word **'and'** leads to reading by analogy, e.g. h**and,** s**and,** b**and.**

- Use wooden/plastic letters for children to interchange onsets: **p**en/**h**en/**m**en.

Develop an awareness of blends and digraphs

- Try to teach common digraphs **'sh', 'ch',** and **'th'** when introducing letter sounds. Contrast the difference in sound between **s/sh, jkh, f/th**. Give the children examples of the difference in meaning simply by the change of sound, e.g. **sue/shoe, jug/chug, fin/thin**.

- Teach blends thoroughly. Play lots of games that help children to gain an accurate knowledge and solid foundation to develop their word blending skills further.

- Ask children to 'track' blends on a page of print. They should use a highlighter pen and mark each time the blend appears. Encourage role reversal in games and activities.

Comprehension of language

Comprehension of language is also known as 'understanding' or 'receptive' language.

The following shows a normal pattern of language development and may prove a useful guideline when working with children with delayed language:

12 months–18 months

- Points to familiar objects on request, e.g. 'Where is teddy?' 'Where's the car?' etc.
- Follows simple commands, e.g. 'Get your coat', 'Shut the door', etc.
- Is able to show own or doll's hair, hands, shoes, etc.
- Demonstrates definitions by use, e.g. brush own hair.

2–3 Years

- Understands function of objects and can identify simple objects by use, e.g. 'What do we cut with?'
- Acts on simple commands with 2 key words, e.g. 'Put the box on the chair' (where there is an alternative to 'box' and 'chair').
- Can match objects to pictures.
- Can relate meaningfully to miniature toys.

3 Years

- Acts upon 3–4 key words instructions, e.g. 'Put the book under the chair.' 'Put the teddy under the bed.' (where an alternative is provided to the underlined objects).
- Understands concepts big/little/in/on/under.
- Understands some reference to past and future events.
- Understands attributes of objects, e.g. 'Which man has the biggest hat?'
- Listens to stories of increasing length.

4 Years

- Understanding less based in the Present, shows more developed understanding of past and future tenses.
- Acts upon 4+ key word instructions, e.g. 'Put the red crayon in the little box' (where an alternative is provided to the underlined objects).
- Understands concepts such as behind/in front of and long/short.
- Can identify some colours.

5 Years

- Can understand everyday conversations.
- Understands and follows more complex instructions.
- Concept of time starts to develop, e.g. 'today', 'tomorrow' and 'yesterday'.

Problems arising from comprehension difficulties

The following problems may be due to difficulties with understanding spoken language. These problems may also, to varying degrees, be caused by:

Poor auditory memory
Sequencing difficulties
Immaturity of attention control.

- Difficulty following instructions.
- Unable to follow story or to answer questions, for example in the Literacy Hour.
- Expressive language affected: may lack vocabulary or have problems with grammar and syntax.
- May find it hard to concentrate in class or to sit still.
- May be able to read accurately, but can lack understanding of text.
- May appear to have behaviour difficulties.
- May have poor self-esteem; may find it hard to socialise with other children.

Elements of language

Understanding may break down because children have difficulty with the following (difficulties here will also be reflected in the child's spoken language):

Vocabulary

Learnt through context and experience. Children with vocabulary difficulties miss out on the building bricks of later language development.

Semantics

An understanding of how words link and relate to each other and how context affects words. For example, the different meanings of 'light' in the phrases 'light green' and 'a light load'.

Syntax

Following and understanding structure and word order of sentences. For example, the different meanings of 'the man pushed the horse' and the more complex 'the man is being pushed by the horse'.

Morphology

The smallest element of meaning in a word, such as the 's' in 'hats' as opposed to 'hat' or the 'ed' in 'walked' as opposed to 'walk'. These endings change the meaning of language, but may not be understood by a child with comprehension difficulty.

General strategies to help improve language comprehension

- Use child's name and establish eye contact before speaking.

- Encourage active listening (see 'Listening Skills' section).

- Ensure that activities are appropriate for child's level of development, e.g. use real objects in preference to line drawings for younger children.

- When teaching verbs, ask the children to perform the actions and to use the words that describe them.

- Use everyday objects that reflect the child's experience.

- Vary objects and activities to maintain interest.

- Ensure a lot of practice and reinforcement of new vocabulary and concepts.

- Use in a variety of situations to encourage the child to generalise skills. Remember, it may take a long time to learn new concepts and words.

- Adult's speech should be clear and unhurried, with normal intonation.

- Keep sentences short, if necessary broken into separate parts.

- Re-phrase sentences.

- Allow time for the child to respond.

- When reading with the child, talk about the story; ask what? where? or who? questions to establish understanding.

- At a higher level, ask why? how? or when? questions about stories, objects or events.

- Use role play to help children understand why or when they are having difficulty understanding. For example, play a barrier game and do not give the child all the necessary information to complete a task.

- Encourage the child to tell you when they do not understand.

- Offer a range of options: ask for clarification, use a dictionary, re-read a text (looking at contextual cues) or ask a neighbour.

- Use visual cues to support spoken information and, if appropriate, use gesture or signing to accompany language.

Visual supports

Children who experience difficulties with communication may need visual strategies to aid their understanding. Images can provide a two-way communication path for anyone who has limited verbal abilities.

Tod and Blamires (1998) suggest that learners may need to have the following visual cues emphasised as they may not be able to make as much use of them as accomplished communicators.

Body language
e.g. facial expression, body posture and proximity, touching, eye contact, direction and shifting of gaze.

Environmental cues
e.g. signs, labels, written messages, instructions, notes, furniture arrangement, location and movement of people and objects.

Tools for giving information and helping organisation
e.g. calendars, daily planners, schedules, shopping lists, notes, menus, maps.

Specially designed tools for specific needs
✓ *Schedules and mini-schedules* – outlining the day or part of the day. They may be for all the class to use or for a specific child who may have the schedule by his/her desk.

✓ *Choice boards* – showing a range of choices.

✓ *Task organisers* – step by step prompts to help a learner complete a task. This may include individualised worksheets that show what the task is, what materials are required, the stages of the task and how it will be finished. It is recommended that traditionally established organising principles be used to structure tasks, e.g. left to right and top down.

Label prompts in the environment
Support may be required to help the child make use of existing visual cues, e.g. exit signs, toilets, etc. The child may need the additional support of labelling areas and items. Having a place for everything and returning it to its place can be made more explicit through the use of additional labelled containers and/or marked out areas or boundaries, e.g. the carpeted area is a place for listening to stories or reading quietly.

Digital photographs
Digital cameras are useful as a quick and relatively simple way of providing photographs. These can be used as a guide to an activity or task showing each stage or just the completion. Photographs need to indicate the key element to be considered.

Visual communication links
Lists/pictures that communicate information from one setting to another, e.g. between home and school.

Overlay keyboards for computers and on-screen grids
Computer software, e.g. Clicker and Concept, can provide visual and spoken prompts for writing and learning activities (see 'Resources' section).

Picture or object exchange systems
This involves exchange of a picture or object referring to a desired item with the teacher, who immediately responds to the request. An example of a picture communication system is *PECS* or *Picture Exchange Communication System* (see 'Resources' section).

Expressive language (spoken)

The following shows a normal pattern of expressive or spoken language development:

12 months–18 months
- Child uses 2–20 recognisable words.
- Uses one word to express whole idea.
- May use echolalia, i.e. echoes last or prominent word said to him/her.
- Communicates wishes by pointing.

2–3 Years
- Vocabulary increases to 200+ but speech will show signs of immature sentence structure or phonology (sound system).
- What? where? and who? questions are emerging.
- Uses simple 2–3 word sentences, e.g. 'Daddy kick ball.'
    'Put dolly bath.'

3–4 Years
- Sentences become more complex: using prepositions, adjectives, plurals and some use of past tense.
- Starting to ask why? when? and who? questions.
- Can carry on simple conversations.
- Is able to talk about recent events and experiences.
- Can recite simple nursery rhymes.
- Will play imaginatively and comment on what is happening.
- May experience periods of normal non-fluency in speech production.

4–5 Years
- Sentences grammatically correct and intelligible.
- A few speech substitutions remain (e.g. /r/ to /w/ and /th/ to /f/).
- Can give a connected account of recent events and experiences.
- Knows various rhymes and jingles.
- Enjoys jokes and playing with language.
- Often asks why/what/where/when/how? questions
- Likes to ask the meanings of words.

5 Years

- Speech is fluent, grammatically correct and usually phonetically correct.
- Enjoys singing and reciting nursery rhymes.
- Constantly asking the meaning of abstract words and using them with delight.
- Enjoys jokes and riddles.

Problems arising

- Child may be withdrawn and isolated.

- May have difficulty establishing friendships.

- May have poor eye contact and turn-taking skills.

- May be frustrated and appear to have behaviour difficulties.

- Sentence structure may appear immature; word order may be confused.

- May use gesture and 'empty' words such as 'that' or 'thingy'.

- Unable to join in class discussions or to answer questions.

- Will be unable to make needs or worries known.

- May have literacy difficulties as written language will reflect spoken language.

- May have difficulty with prediction, sequencing and inference.

General strategies to help expressive language difficulties

- Check hearing.

- Check child's understanding.

- Observe the child, see where and when s/he talks spontaneously.

- The child may need a warm, close relationship with an adult to encourage him/her to talk.

- Do not expect spontaneous talk in all situations until confident in familiar ones.

- Use concrete objects and familiar events and objects to talk about.

- Give the child full attention when s/he wants to speak.

- Give child time to talk.

- Record samples of the child's language and where appropriate complete an assessment (see 'Resources' section for suggestions on assessments). Seek specialist help if appropriate.

- Comment on activities, talk while playing or working alongside the child, encourage communication.

- Use corrective feedback, but do not pressurise the child to repeat what may be difficult.

- Use signing or gesture to augment communication.

- Use categorisation to help child develop word-finding skills.

Specific strategies to develop expressive language skills

The following techniques can be used to elicit specific vocabulary or sentence structures:

- ✔ Modelled imitation
- ✔ Forced alternatives
- ✔ Indirect modelling
- ✔ Cloze procedure
- ✔ Expansion
- ✔ Role reversal
- ✔ Obstacle presentation

Modelled imitation

- The adult models language for the child to imitate, for example:
  If you would like juice say 'juice please'.
- Use the language to be copied at the end of the sentence to help memory.
- Signs can be used to accompany language where necessary.

Forced alternatives

This will give the child vocabulary that is needed, but is not simple imitation:

N.B. The target phrase or word should always be given first to avoid the child simply echoing the last word they heard.

(a) Help with word-finding retrieval, e.g.:
Adult: **What colour is the apple?**
Child: No response.
Adult: **Is it green or blue?**
Child: **Green.**

(b) Help with incorrect productions, e.g.:
Child: **Me want a turn.**
Adult: **Do you say me want a turn or I want a turn?**
Child: **I want a turn.**

(c) Help with expanding sentence structure, e.g.:
Child: **Girl eat.**
Adult: **Is it girl eating an apple or girl eating a cake?**
Child: **Girl eat cake.**

Indirect modelling

Here the adult produces a statement in such a way as to provide the child indirectly with the words s/he will need.

This relies on the child actively analysing the model and reproducing it or aspects of it in their speech.

It is useful for prompting passive children into making requests, e.g.:

Adult: **If you want more juice, ask me.**

Child: **Want more juice.**

Adult: **Tell me if you need a pencil.**

Child: **Need pencil.**

Adult: **If you ask me, where is the rubber? I will tell you.**

Child: **Where is the rubber?**

Cloze procedure

Here the adult models a sentence and prompts the child to use a similar sentence but with a different vocabulary:

Two pictures: a boy eating a cake and a girl eating an apple.

Adult: **This is a girl eating an apple and this is...**

Child: **Boy eat cake.**

Adult: **I'm sitting on a big chair and you're sitting...**

Child: **On little chair.**

Expansion

The adult reinforces and expands upon what the child has said. The aim is not for the child to reproduce the adult's expanded version but to experience language at a slightly higher level than they have been using, e.g.:

Child: **Daddy car.**

Adult: **That's right, daddy's gone in the car.**

Child: **We wented to the park.**

Adult: **Yes, we went to the park yesterday.**

Role reversal

Here the adult models the language first. Then the adult and child swap roles and the child is encouraged to use the same or similar commands, e.g.:

Adult: **Put the teddy in the box.**

Put the pencil under the table, etc.

(Adult then says to the child, 'Now you tell me what to do'.)

Obstacle presentation

The adult sets up a situation which forces the child to make some form of comment or request, e.g.:

The adult gives the child a puzzle to complete, but some pieces are missing.

The adult asks the child to cut out a picture, but does not provide any scissors.

Social communication difficulties in children

Some children have difficulty with understanding and using language effectively to communicate. They may have problems in the following areas:

- The child has difficulty interacting with peers and may appear to be detached from the group.
- The child's expressive language may be in advance of their understanding.
- The child's language or responses may, however, appear inappropriate at times; s/he may change topic without warning or use stereotyped utterances.
- The child may not have naturally absorbed the norms of social etiquette. For example, s/he may talk to adults in an over-familiar way, may stand too close to another person or inappropriately touch them.
- The child may find turn-taking difficult in: conversation, e.g. may talk over another and not listen to questions; games/activities, e.g. may be unwilling to share, dislike losing.
- The child may experience difficulty with eye contact and inattention may be a problem. S/he may fail to pick up on non-verbal cues, such as facial expression or tone of voice, e.g. the child may not realise that someone who is frowning is annoyed.
- The child may learn to read at an early age, but s/he may have a poor understanding of what s/he has read.
- The child may have difficulty with inference and predicting and seeing things from another person's perspective.
- The child may fail to see the overall picture and tend to concentrate on the smaller details instead.
- The child's language may be highly literal so that sarcasm, jokes and idioms are not clearly understood, e.g. 'Pull your socks up'.
- The child may have difficulty with abstract language and time concepts, e.g. child may be confused if s/he is told 'you can play a game when you have finished your work' (see 'Resources' section for recommendations).

General strategies to help children with social communication difficulties

- Listen to the child, giving time to talk, do not answer on his/her behalf.

- Give gentle reminders if communication skills have broken down.

- Talk about events or difficulties as they arise.

- Guide the child towards solving his/her own problems.

- Talk about how the child is feeling and how others may feel in a given situation.

- Give the child choices and let him/her tell you which s/he wants.

- Use visual cues and prompts where possible.

- Use real objects and materials wherever appropriate to demonstrate.

Specific activities to help children with social communication difficulties

Early Years and Key Stage 1

The young child with social communication difficulties may appear to be talking well; much of his/her language, however, may be simply memorised chunks, used without full understanding. The child needs to start using language to communicate. The following recommendations are taken from *Semantic-Pragmatic Language Disorder* by **Firth & Venkatesh** (see 'Resource' section) and provides very useful practical strategies:

Following and giving instructions

An important area for understanding the language of the classroom.

- Play Simon Says or other PE activities, where child has to run, jump, stop, stand still, etc. on request. In appropriate situations, child can instruct adult or group of children.

- Play alongside child with toys, instruct child to 'put dolly's hat on' or to 'put teddy's shoes on'. Keep language simple, expand as child's understanding develops. Reverse roles and child instructs adult.

- Child and adult have identical drawing, barrier between the two. Adult instructs child to add/colour objects on picture; compare the pictures to see accuracy of results. Reverse roles and child instructs adult.

Confirming and refuting (saying yes/no)

Some children find this hard and have a tendency to say 'yes' to everything you ask them.

- Pick up objects and ask the child, 'is this an apple?' etc.

- Sort coloured cubes, asking the child if a cube is a certain colour or not.

- Sort items belonging to different people, 'is this Sam's?' etc.

Requesting and listening to requests

Again a vital area if the child is to function in the classroom and interact with peers.

- Play fishing game, where child has to request specific items and retrieve them. Reverse roles.

- Play at shopping; ask the child for items; develop level of complexity from 'cake please' to 'please can I have a cake' when appropriate. Child takes turn at being shopkeeper.

- Play game together; adult asks for parts of jigsaw/construction toy and encourages child to do the same.

Asking and answering questions

An understanding of 'wh' questions is vital in the development of understanding language.

- Child hides a toy in the room and adult asks questions about its whereabouts; child and adult then reverse roles.

- Give the child a choice of drinks or biscuits and ask which s/he would like. Allow the child to give out food or drink to group and to ask the children what they want.

- Use a feely bag and encourage the child to ask what things are; ask questions about what an object feels like, etc.

- Look at a picture book together and ask the child questions about what s/he can see, for example, 'where is the boy?' etc.

Turn-taking skills

This is an important pre-linguistic skill and one which some children need to learn specifically.

- Play circle activities, pass round a bean bag and ask the child to say his/her name while holding the bean bag. Increase complexity of language when appropriate.

- Play dice/board games, at first adult and child and then, if appropriate, with two or three children. Ensure that each child takes turns, ask at intervals, 'whose turn is it next?'

Specific grammatical areas

In order to develop a child's language, it may be useful to focus on specific areas. This will encourage the child to start using language appropriately, rather than simply repeating memorised chunks.

- **Nouns:** Ask the child to name objects, photos or pictures; this can be done in a game context, such as fishing, lotto or shopping.

- **Verbs:** Ask the child to perform certain actions and to describe what actions others are doing. Use verb photos or pictures as nouns, above.

- **Adjectives:** Feel and describe toys, such as 'fluffy cat', 'soft teddy' or 'bouncy ball'.

- **Prepositions:** Use small toys and place items in/on/under another, e.g. 'put the shoes in the cupboard', 'put the doll under the bed', etc.

Key Stage 2

The child now needs to learn to communicate with other children as well as adults. The previous activities for Key Stage 1 started to use these skills and the child would now benefit from wider experience with peers.

Turn-taking and verbal and non-verbal communication skills

Develop the ideas used in circle time activities for younger children:

- Take it in turns in circle time to talk about such topics as food, family, pets, etc.
- When children are more confident in circle time, talk about feelings and emotions in different situations, e.g. 'how do you feel when you are going to the dentist/cinema, get a present', etc.

Rules of conversation

Just as other children need to be taught reading and spelling, so some will need to be taught the rules of conversation, as they do not pick them up incidentally.

- Two adults can act out a conversation, making a series of mistakes, which the children have to spot, for example:
    - Talking too fast.
    - Not listening to other person/talking over them.
    - Not looking at other person.
    - Standing too close to the other person.
    - Changing the subject too often and without warning.

The children can then devise a list of conversational rules that will serve as a reminder for them at a later date.

Using appropriate language/questions

The following activities will help the child to use language accurately and appropriately:

- Use barrier games, as for younger children, but with instructions of increasing complexity. Instead of a child and an adult, two children can work together, taking it in turns to instruct the other person.
- One child instructs another to draw a similar picture, for example, of a monster/alien. They compare drawings afterwards to see how successful they have been.
- One child hides an object and the second child has to ask appropriate questions to find out where it is.

Using appropriate language/questions (continued)

- One child has a picture of an object and the other has to work out what it is from a series of questions, for example 'where do you find it?' or 'who would use it?' etc.
- As above, but this time the questions can only be answered 'yes' or 'no'. For example, 'is it alive?' or 'is it an animal?' etc. This will encourage the children to think in terms of categories and classification.

Inference and prediction

These activities will encourage children to think of language in terms other than the literal and the concrete.

- In story sessions/Literacy Hour encourage the child to predict what will happen in a story.
- Ask 'why' s/he feels something has happened, for example, 'Why is Sam wearing a coat and hat?' (because it is cold).
- Encourage the child to relate to the feelings of others through story: 'How do you think Sam felt when he saw his friend fall out of the tree?' Help the child to find words for emotions beyond simply 'happy' or 'sad'.
- Use sequence pictures, but with the final picture not revealed. Talk about the events in the pictures and ask the child to suggest what might happen next.

Understanding of time/sequencing

The concept of time is a complex one for many children to appreciate, particularly those children with social communication difficulties.

- The child may benefit from a visual timetable where each activity of the day is represented in picture form. When an activity is finished, it could be placed in the 'finished box' (see section on 'Visual supports').
- As the child becomes more familiar with this, clock faces could be put next to each activity to show when each was (theoretically) going to happen.
- Questions could be asked, such as 'At what time do we do PE?' or 'What do we do after assembly?'
- Take photographs of the child in a series of actions, for example, coming into school, hanging up coat, putting away packed lunch, going into classroom and sitting down. Use these to generate language and the idea of sequenced activities.
- Use commercially produced sequence cards, as above. Ask the child, for example, 'What happens in the first picture/after the boy got home/what did he do before he saw the dog?' etc.
- Carry out a task that requires a sequence of actions, for example, making a sandwich; talk about what was done, make picture representations and ask the child to make a sandwich following the picture cues.
- For time concepts involving longer passages of time, such as the growth of plants, show the children stages of growth at one time, for example, the hyacinth bulb in the soil, the pot with the small shoot, the taller shoot and the flower in bloom. Ask them to put the pots in sequence. Talk about how long it would take for the plant to grow.

Specific grammatical areas

The children may need to practise the following:

Past tense:

- Ask the children to close their eyes and listen to the adult performing an action, such as clapping hands. They then open their eyes and say what happened: 'you clapped your hands', etc.
- Use picture sequences to describe, where the child has to tell what has happened in the pictures, e.g. 'he picked the flowers', etc.
- In the Literacy Hour, ask the child to tell what has happened in a story, modelling language where necessary.

Future tense:

- Show the children a half-completed action, such as a ball about to be kicked, a door about to be shut. Say to the children, 'what will I do?' and they should say, 'you are going to shut the door'. Once again, the language may need to be modelled and the children encouraged not simply to answer, 'shut the door'.
- Use sequencing cards/pictures and ask the children what is going to happen.

Adjectives:

- Develop understanding and use of adjectives by using feely bags, where the child has to describe what they can feel.
- Alternatively, the children ask the child who is touching the object what it feels like: 'Is it soft/hard?' etc.
- Play a board game – when the child lands on a certain square, they have to think of/find an object that is: heavy, red, wooden, soft, etc.

Building vocabulary

Many children lack a breadth of vocabulary or have word-finding difficulties. They would benefit from the following. Categorisation games:

- Play a game where the children have to collect pictures from a certain category. Talk about the category and think of other objects from it.
- The adult thinks of a category – children name items from that category.
- Collect pairs of items/pictures of items that go together, such as knife and fork, toothpaste and toothbrush; talk about why they go together.
- Ask the child to select the odd one out from a series of items/pictures. This involves the child understanding categorisation in order to understand and then explain why an item is different from the rest.

Circle time

Circle time is a time for children to gather together to share their ideas and feelings and to discuss matters of significance.

It can provide a good opportunity for helping children with language difficulties to develop the following areas:

- ✔ Attention control
- ✔ Turn-taking skills
- ✔ Eye contact
- ✔ Social interaction
- ✔ Self-esteem
- ✔ Good listening
- ✔ Good speaking
- ✔ Good thinking

To do this, it is important to establish ground rules:

Ground rules for circle time

- Everyone is equal (it helps if you all sit at the same level).
- Everyone should have the chance to speak (it may help to pass around an object for the speaker to hold).
- Each person has a responsibility to listen.
- Everyone shows respect for another's point of view.
- Children have a right not to speak if they so wish.
- Children should not be penalised when they choose not to speak.
- Children should not be excluded from circle time for previous inappropriate behaviour.

The teacher will need to:

- Set the rules as above, which are, in essence, good listening skills, with respect for others' points of view.
- Find a suitable time.
- Praise good listening skills.
- Explain that what is talked about in circle time is confidential.
- Plan variety within the sessions; introduce enjoyable routines to start and end with.
- Build self-evaluation into the circle time.

Activities for circle time

There are several publications which provide ideas for circle time activities, for example, *Language Development: Circle Time Sessions to Improve Communication Skills* by Nash, Lowe and Palmer, and for secondary pupils, *Quality Circle Time in the Secondary School: A Handbook of Good Practice* by Mosley and Tew.

As a general rule, where a circle time activity involves talking, pass round an object such as a beanbag or a soft toy, which the speaker can hold. Activities can include some of the following:

Sentence completion
- 'My name is...'
- 'I like to...'
- 'My favourite lesson is...'

Passing an action. Pass around a clap or series of claps.
- Stand up in turn around the circle.
- Look at the person next to you in turn.
- Pass around you a smile.
- Decide on a feeling, such as 'happy' or 'angry' and pass around a face to go with that feeling. This is a useful activity for children with social communication difficulties.

Passing an object
- Passing a beanbag or ball around the circle is a simple and effective warm up activity for children with difficulties with turn-taking or immature attention control.
- Joining hands and passing a hula hoop around the circle (either over heads or under feet) is a good team building activity which requires the group to work together.

Discussing topics
- Talk about areas of interest or concern to the group, such as bullying or school rules.
- For older children, this might include topics such as politics, drugs and alcohol.

Problem-solving
- Some children have used circle time as a useful opportunity to talk about problems that have arisen.
- Differences can be talked about and possible solutions aired as a group.
- Stories can be used to refer to ways of dealing with problems.

Citizenship through circle time

The Citizenship Curriculum became statutory in British secondary schools in September 2002.

Circle time offers a very useful opportunity to put the ideals of citizenship into practice. It models the qualities that the curriculum seeks to promote.

Circle time can offer children with speech and language difficulties the opportunity to practise skills they may have problems with and to see those skills modelled by other children.

These include:
- Co-operation and turn-taking.
- Active and supportive listening.
- Sharing and managing feelings.
- Affirmation of self and others. Developing empathy.
- Communicating ideas and opinions.
- Voting on issues. Considering some political and topical issues.
- Making real choices and decisions, such as school rules, in the class and the playground.
- Looking at the qualities of friendship.
- Reflective thinking. Setting and reviewing goals.
- Considering moral dilemmas. Taking action.

Speech acquisition

A normally developing pattern of speech acquisition would be broadly as follows:

Age	Sounds acquired
18 months	m n p b t d w and vowels
2–2.5 years	As above plus k g ng h and vowels
2–3.5 years	Starting to use f, s, l and y (as in 'you')
3 years	As above plus z l and vowels
4 years	As above plus ch j and vowels
5 years	Starting to develop r th
5 years	Speech fully understandable

Delay or disorder?

A child's speech is considered to be *delayed* when his/her progress follows a normal pattern, but his/her speech sound acquisition is that of a younger child.

A child's phonology is considered *disordered* when the processes used are inconsistent and not following the normal pattern of phonological development (as seen above).

Speech difficulties

School age children whose speech is still unclear in any of the following areas would be considered to be *delayed*:

- **Fronting:** a sound which should be produced at the back of the mouth is made further forward:

    Cat can become **tat**

    Get can become **det**

    Sing can become **sin** or **sim**.

- **Stopping of fricatives:** the longer fricative sounds (f, v, s, z, sh, th) become short plosive sounds (p, b, t, d, k):

    Sun can become **tun**

    Fan can become **pan**.

- **Cluster reduction:** the child leaves out consonant sounds from a cluster, most commonly l, r or s:

    Skate can become **Kate** or **sate**

    Spot can become **pot** or **sot**.

- **Final consonant deletion:** here the final consonant is not sounded:

    Tent can become **ten**

    Milk can become **mil**.

The following is **not** part of normal development and would be considered a possible indication of a **language disorder**.

- **Backing:** the opposite of fronting; the sound is made further back in the mouth:

    Pan can become **can**

    Tap can become **cap**

    Bet can become **get**.

Points to note when working with children with speech difficulties

- If a child has speech problems, it is very important to refer him/her to a speech and language therapist who can discuss the difficulties.

- Establishing links between the school, home and the therapist is a useful way of using different people's skills and knowledge. It is the most effective way of helping the child.

- It is important to establish the child's ability to discriminate between sounds as this is necessary before s/he can alter his/her own production.

- Do remember that a child who has phonological problems will not be able to use sounds which are beyond his/her developmental level (see chart, above).

- The child may not be consistent in sound substitution. If this is the case or if many sounds are affected, then his/her speech may be very difficult to understand.

- The difficulty the child has with particular sounds may depend on that sound's position within a word and on the sounds adjacent to it. For example, s/he may be able to sound /k/ in 'cup', but cannot sound in 'back'.

Classroom strategies for helping children with speech difficulties

A. Locke and M. Beech in *Teaching Talking* recommend the following:

- Check the child's hearing.

- Check understanding.

- Listen to the child; his/her speech will become more comprehensible with familiarity.

- Remember to use context and present experience.

- Encourage the child to watch and listen to the person talking to them.

- Encourage the child to talk slowly in short sentences.

- Avoid allowing the child to talk on and on; try asking questions to help clarify what s/he wants to say.

- Encourage the child to make him/herself understood by using gesture, drawings, own signs, etc.

- Do not ask the child to repeat what s/he has said or to say a particular word properly.

Language in the NLS

Literacy unites the important skills of reading and writing. It also involves speaking and listening, which although they are not separately identified in the framework, are an essential part of it. Good oral work enhances pupils' understanding of language in both oral and written forms and of the way language can be used to communicate. (DfEE 1998)

Speaking and listening is the foundation of written work. Children need to be able to use language orally before they can be expected to produce it in written form. They need to be able to use language to develop their thinking and reasoning skills and to access the curriculum.

In view of this the QCA has issued guidance entitled. *Speaking, Listening, Learning: Working with Children in Key Stages 1 and 2* **(2003). This document looks at language across the curriculum and sets objectives for speaking and listening in Years 1 to 6.**

The following recommendations will help to provide ideas for the Literacy Strategy.

Strategies for developing spoken language in the Literacy Strategy

- Sit the child near you where s/he can follow the visual cues of other children.
- Use the child's name frequently.
- Encourage good eye contact.
- Gain the child's full attention when engaged in talk or discussion (see section on 'Teaching "Active Listening"').
- Use simple sentences; avoid complicated sentence structures, such as the passive or abstract vocabulary and concepts.
- Encourage the child, where appropriate, to answer in full sentences

    e.g.   Teacher: 'Where is the dog hiding?'

              Child: 'The dog is hiding under the table.'
- Using object prompts will help promote greater understanding, e.g. story sacks or any objects or artefacts which are part of the text.
- Picture prompts will also help understanding and will support new vocabulary.
- Relate the text to the children's experience whenever possible.
- Use varied strategies, such as direct modelling or forced alternatives to elicit responses from the child (see Expressive Language section on 'Specific Strategies to Develop Expressive Language Skills').

- Circle time can be incorporated into the Literacy Strategy by using the second 15 minutes for developing either:
- ✔ skills such as turn-taking, eye contact and social interaction;
- ✔ specific speech and language objectives
- Allow the child the opportunity to develop their language. This will involve giving them time to reply and perhaps, at times, suppressing more vocal class members.
- The child who is hesitant may prefer to whisper their answer to a child support assistant before they talk to the whole class.
- Ensure that 'wh' questions are used appropriately.

A useful reference which looks at the details of the different ways in which children use language can be found in the Appendix (Profiles of language use in Nursery and Key Stages 1 & 2, taken from Ann Locke and Maggie Beech's *Teaching Talking*).

Use of questions

'Wh' questions are vital for an understanding of the language of the classroom. For the child with language difficulties, it is better to start with simpler questions, such as:

> **'What?'**   e.g. 'What is in the tree?' (bird)
>   'What is the girl doing?' (girl running)
> The expected answer can be a noun or a verb or a simple phrase.
>
> **'Where?'**   e.g. 'Where is the man?' (in the car)
> Encourage the child not simply to point or answer 'there', but to use early prepositions, such as in/on/under, etc.
>
> **'Who?'**   e.g. 'Who has a big ice cream?' (Sam)

When the child can understand the above, you can move on to:

> **'Why?'**   e.g. 'Why is the boy crying?' (he fell over)
>
> **'How?'**   e.g. 'How do we know it's raining outside?' (because he's wet)
>
> **'When?'**   e.g. 'When do we go on the computer?' (after play)

Written language in the Literacy Strategy

Children with spoken language difficulties may have strong visual skills and these can be used to good advantage.

- Give the child the object they are to write about, let them look at it and feel it to help generate language.

- Use simple picture sequences as a framework for writing. Ask the child to sequence the pictures and to talk about what is happening in them.

- Use computers to generate picture sequences, where the child can either match sentences to pictures or write their own sentences.

Children with language difficulties can benefit greatly from developing their reading skills; this will provide them with a starting point from which comprehension and language use can be extended.

- Use high frequency words to generate sentences which can, in turn, develop spoken language skills:

  e.g.   'I can...'

  'I like...'

  'I can see a...' etc.

- Use the child's own reading book to enhance the child's use of language. Develop skills such as understanding of cause and effect, empathy and ability to predict or imagine. This will be particularly important for children with social communication difficulties (see section on 'Social Communication').

Language in the National Numeracy Strategy

Oral work is a key feature of the National Numeracy Strategy (NNS).

The Strategy recommends a balance of whole class teaching and group work, with talk playing a central role in the learning process.

> ### Do remember:
>
> Many children with language and learning difficulties have problems with **sequencing**, which is vital for the development of mathematical concepts.
>
> They may also have problems understanding **cause and effect**, which is another important area in mathematical understanding.
>
> Children with problems of **short-term auditory memory** will have difficulty with mental maths. They may need to develop prompts and strategies to help them, such as visualising or using their fingers.
>
> Children with language difficulties will need time and a lot of practice in order to acquire a **mathematical vocabulary**.

✔ Ensure that the child understands what s/he is being asked to do. For the child with language difficulties, **concepts** such as more and less, before and after, smaller and larger than, may need explaining and lots of practical activities carried out before knowledge becomes secure.

✔ Ensure that **vocabulary**, as well as concepts, is familiar, so that the children know, for example, what a triangle, or a corner, or a side is. Use appropriate displays, with visual prompts, for the children to refer to during lessons.

✔ When asking the whole class a question, build in enough **'wait time'** to allow all children to think of their answer. Ask the whole class to repeat a correct answer, using a **complete sentence**.

✔ Wherever possible, allow the child access to **concrete apparatus** so that s/he can develop concepts and vocabulary through practical experience.

✔ An **'empty number line'** helps children to structure and record mental processes. It is a useful aid to short-term memory.

✔ Try to relate learning to **real life experience**, so that maths is not seen as simply a school subject, but rather as something of practical and everyday use.

The management of communication problems in the classroom

(strategies taken from *Teaching Talking* – A. Locke & M. Beech)

Regular use of appropriate management strategies can be very beneficial in fostering communication skills in children.

General management strategies for *all* children identified with problems in communication:

Increasing confidence
a) Relationships with adults
b) Relationships with other children
c) Being successful

a) Relationships with adults
- Make a point of having a relaxed 'chat' with the child.
- Chat during practical activities.
- Adults should always pause to show they would welcome a response from the child.

b) Relationships with other children
- Put the child with others who communicate well but who will not dominate the conversation.

c) Being successful
- Develop all skills but especially where the child shows special interest or ability.
- Regularly show appreciation of the child's effort.

Helping communication in the classroom
a) Noise level
b) Context
c) Watching and listening
d) Other children
e) Parents
f) Repetition
g) Collecting background information

a) Noise level
- Have quiet areas in the classroom where the child can spend part of the day listening or talking with an adult with or without other children.

b) Context
- Shared context and experiences are easier to talk about than events that are only known to one person.

c) Watching and listening
- Encourage the child to give eye contact.
- Encourage the child to watch as well as listen.
- Say name to gain attention.

d) Other children
- Can be helpful by repeating instructions, explaining or demonstrating tasks.
  N.B. Care should be taken that someone else does not always talk for the child.

e) Parents
- Share information from home so that school can talk about home experiences
- A home–school book may be useful – messages can be written, pictures drawn and interesting events described.

f) Repetition
- Rhymes, poems, songs thus attending to speech patterns, new vocabulary and language structures.
- Learning to listen well to stories.

g) Collecting background information
- Outside agencies, e.g. speech therapy, medical, etc.

Individual Education Plans

Schools need to give greater attention, not so much to the specific detail of the IEP, but how it relates to teacher planning. (Ofsted 1997).

What is on the Individual Education Plan (IEP) is not the only matter for concern: it is how the IEP is going to be implemented that is important.

Speech and language permeates the whole curriculum, indeed the whole school day. This means there are many opportunities to develop a child's speech and language.

Good planning can help to do this more effectively.

Useful starting points might be:

> **When** is the best time to target specific language areas?
> **Who** can best work with the child?

The following suggestions give examples of how to incorporate language targets into the curriculum.

Do remember:

It is important for the adult to secure the child's attention first and to give instructions in short, clear chunks.

- Story in the Literacy Hour (with the teacher)

Listening to and talking about a story can help develop:

- ✔ Attention control
- ✔ Listening skills
- ✔ Turn-taking
- ✔ Eye contact
- ✔ Ability to respond appropriately to 'wh' questions
- ✔ Reasoning skills, an understanding of cause and effect, empathy and the ability to infer and predict.

- Group work in the Literacy Hour (with teacher or CSA)

This does not need to be written work, but can be directed to the needs of the children involved.

- ✔ Circle time (see section on 'Circle Time')
- ✔ Specific language activities in small group
- ✔ Link language and literacy targets (see section on 'Language in the National Literacy Strategy').

- Other curriculum areas (with class teacher/CSA support)

Language skills can be developed in all curriculum areas; this is effective because it means that language can be used more naturally and in context. It also means that a multi-sensory approach can be used and that objects and actions can be explored while language and concepts are developed.

PE

✔ Memory and sequencing skills can be developed through a series of movements and actions.

✔ The children's knowledge of verbs can be developed – running, jumping, crawling, etc.

✔ Parts of the body can be learnt – 'touch your knees', 'stand on one leg with your hands on your hips'.

✔ Specific concepts can be targeted, such as fast and slow, high and low, etc.

✔ A knowledge of colours can be developed – 'run to a red ring', 'pick up a blue beanbag'.

Science and Maths

✔ There are many concepts that can be worked on, for example: colours, hot and cold, light and heavy, more and less, longer and shorter.

- Around the classroom (teacher or CSA)

✔ Giving instructions of increasing length will help develop the children's auditory memory skills, e.g. 'Put the ruler in the tray, your book in your drawer, and line up at the door'.

✔ Giving instructions of increasing grammatical complexity will help develop the children's understanding of language, e.g. 'Put the pencils on my desk and the books in the box under my desk'.

N.B. First make sure that the child understands simple concepts and can follow simple instructions.

- Individual session (with SENSS teacher or CSA)

For some children, the most effective way to develop certain aspects of speech and language will be in individual sessions. Here, they can work on the targets provided by the Speech and Language Therapist or SENSS teacher (see sample IEPs, below).

A comprehensive list of the way in which children's language can be developed across the curriculum areas can be found in *Teaching Talking* (Ann Locke & Maggie Beech: see 'Resources' section).

Ideas for IEPs

The following IEPs are based on a child from primary school and one from secondary school.

Tommy

Tommy is a little boy in Year 1. He is physically adept and always very cheerful. However, he finds it difficult to work on a task without having an adult with him to keep him focused. During the Literacy Hour he finds it hard to listen to a story without being distracted by what's going on around him. His responses to questions are often inappropriate. His answers tend to be short and his vocabulary non-specific, for example, he uses 'thingy' and 'there' a lot. When working in a group with his peers he has difficulty turn-taking and often interrupts other children.

Jenny

Jenny is a girl in Year 7 who has difficulty with social communication skills. She has problems with auditory memory, which results in her finding it hard to follow instructions. She does, however, have visual strengths, which means that she benefits from having visual prompts. At times she gives inappropriate responses to questions and finds it difficult to give explanations for choices or opinions.

Individual Education Plan

Name: Tommy .... DOB: .... NC Year: 1 .... Stage: ....

Teacher: .... Term: .... Date: .... Next Review Date: ....

Nature of difficulties: Tommy has difficulties with attention, listening and turn-taking skills. His expressive language skills are immature.

P-Level/N.C. Level	Targets	W	A	Strategies/Resources (including use of IT)	Evaluation
Attention	**Attention Control**			Gradually increase length of time & complexity of task.	
P11	Maintains attention to task with some intermittent support.				
				Follow Attention Control Level 4 recommendations.	
AT1	**Listens to stories in Literacy Hour:**				
P6	• Gives appropriate eye contact.			Use of 'active listening' rules promoting 'good listening' skills.	
P6	• Responds to simple questions What? Who? Where? (Focus on developing verbs and extending vocabulary.)				
				During each Literacy Hour session ensure that the child is asked a question and is given the opportunity to ask a question to teacher/child.	
P6	• Asks simple questions What? Who? Where?				
Interaction	**Participates in circle time:**				
				Use of praise, stickers or star chart to reward good turn-taking.	
P7	• Waits for turn to speak.				
AT1					
P7	Listens to others talk by demonstrating good listening skills.			Simple questioning to check 'good listening'.	

57

Individual Education Plan

Name: Jenny .... DOB: .... NC Year: 7 .... Stage: ....

Teacher: .... Term: .... Date: .... Next Review Date: ....

Nature of difficulties: Jenny has problems with social communication skills. She has difficulty interacting with others and with following complex language and lengthy instructions.

P-Level/N.C. Level	Targets	W	A	Strategies/Resources (including use of IT)	Evaluation
2B	To be able to follow instructions in a pair or a group.			✔ Encourage pupils to interact effectively in small groups.	
2B	To be able to ask relevant questions and choose words with precision.			✔ To allow Jenny time to express herself without pressure, within group or class.	
2B	To be able to give reasons for opinions and actions.			✔ To follow timetable with visual as well as written symbols to aid understanding, memory and sequencing skills.	
2B	To be able to demonstrate effective use of visual strategies to support learning, for example, visual timetables, cue cards, etc.				

Support staff: their effective use by teachers

Not all children with speech and language difficulties will require additional support in order to meet their needs within the classroom. For those pupils with a more significant level of need, however, the provision of support staff is vital to ensure that their needs can be met.

Teachers may wish to consider the following when deploying support staff:

- Support staff should promote independence in pupils with whom they are working.
- It may not be necessary to work alongside the pupil in every lesson.
- Allow the pupil to focus on the teacher, rather than on support staff.
- Support staff may need to take notes during teacher input for reference during a later part of the lesson.
- Liaison procedures between home and school should be established under the guidance of the SENCO, Head of Year or form teacher.
- Support service should work under the direction of the SENCO, class or subject teacher.
- Withdrawal of the pupil, in order to follow specific speech and language therapy programmes should be negotiated with the SENCO or teacher.

It is important to remember that the ultimate responsibility for a pupil's access to the curriculum is that of the classroom teacher. Support staff facilitate the delivery of an appropriately differentiated curriculum under the direction of the teacher.

Support staff: initial and ongoing considerations

Support staff should:

Have a clear understanding of their roles and responsibilities:

- have a knowledge of their job description;
- maintain a professional demeanour with parents,
- be aware of school policies with regard to behaviour, anti-bullying, child protection;
- respect the confidentiality of information for all pupils.

Be aware of channels of communication within the school:

- ensure that information given by parents is given to the appropriate member of staff – class teacher, SENCO.
- ensure that communication with outside agencies is carried out in consultation with the SENCO.
- ensure that recommendations and reports from outside agencies are passed to the teacher and SENCO.
- ensure that information given to parents is with the knowledge of the class teacher.
- ensure that there is a mechanism for disseminating information to support staff about school activities, e.g. daily diary, staffroom notice board.

Be recognised as valued members of a team:

- participate in the planning and monitoring process.

Be encouraged to make use of their personal skills:

- share skills, e.g. ICT, creative skills.

Be supported with appropriate on-going professional development:

- observe and learn from other professionals in school and in other establishments.
- undertake training in school and through external courses.

Encourage the pupil's independence at all times:

- promote independent work habits.
- promote independent life skills.
- promote independent play skills.

Support staff: guidelines for working with pupils

Avoid	But instead...
sitting next to the pupil at all times	work with other pupils, while keeping an eye on the pupil you are assigned to
offering too close an oversight during breaks and lunchtimes	encourage playing with peers, introduce games to include others if necessary
collecting equipment for the pupil or putting it away	encourage the pupil to carry this out with independence
completing a task for a pupil	ensure that work is at an appropriate level and is carried out with minimal support (note any support given)
allowing behaviour which is not age-appropriate to the pupil, e.g. holding hands in the playground or in school	encourage the development of more age-appropriate peer relationships by social engineering, 'buddying' or circle of friends
making unnecessary allowances for the pupil	ensure that school rules apply
preventing the pupil from taking the consequences of their actions	insist that the pupil takes the responsibility for and the consequences of his/her actions
tolerating bad behaviour	follow the behaviour policy
making unrealistic demands on the pupil	ensure instructions and work are at the appropriate level
making decisions for the pupil	give the pupil opportunities to make choices and decisions
over-dependency on the support assistant	encourage independent behaviour and work

Working with parents

Parents are increasingly seen as partners with teachers in their child's education. This is particularly true in the area of speech and language, where parents have the opportunity to interact with their child and to develop their language.

Points for parents to remember:

- If you feel you need advice, ask your child's Speech and Language Therapist or teacher for support.

- You do not need to be following a structured programme to develop your child's language.

- Talk about everyday events like cleaning your teeth and washing the dishes.

- Talk about the things you can see on the way to school or playgroup.

- A good time to talk is when you are playing or making something together.

- Above all, make sure your time together is relaxed and enjoyable.

Points for teachers to remember:

- Remember to keep parents updated about their child's progress and to invite them to review meetings.

- Listen to their concerns and trust their knowledge of their child.

- Parents should be aware of the Code of Practice and what it means for their child.

- Encourage them to help in school, for example, with reading, cooking, etc.

- Use a home–school liaison book to talk about events; this will be particularly useful where a child's speech/language is difficult to understand.

Glossary

Articulators

Parts of the vocal apparatus, such as the palate, tongue or voice box.

Attention Control

The ability to focus on stimuli when requested or required, for example, being able to listen to teacher's instructions while writing.

Auditory Discrimination

The ability to notice differences in sounds within words, for example, 'bat' and 'pat', 'kin' and 'king'.

Auditory Short-term Memory

The ability to hold and process information within the working memory resulting in being able, for example, to carry out instructions or blend sounds into a word.

Dysfluency

Inability to control fluency of speech production, resulting in hesitancy, stuttering, etc.

Expressive Language

Using spoken language to communicate.

Grammar/syntax

The rules by which words are combined to produce sentences.

Intonation

Variations in pitch when talking, which may change word meaning.

Morpheme

The smallest unit of meaning which may be a word (as in 'hat' or 'jump') or a word ending; for example, the plural 's' in 'hats', the 'ed' in 'jumped'.

Non-verbal Skills

The ability to communicate without using words, for example, body language, eye contact or gesture.

Phonics

The relationship between speech sounds and letters.

Phonological Awareness

The ability to hear and reflect upon sounds within words, for example an appreciation of rhyme and syllables.

Phonology

The separate sounds within words and the rules that govern the way they occur.

Pragmatics

The aspect of meaning concerned with what someone says and the context in which they say it.

Processing

Understanding what is said and organising what you want to say.

Prosody

The use of intonation, rhythm, speed and volume in language.

Receptive Language

Understanding or comprehension of spoken language.

Semantics

The meanings of words.

Resources

Assessment/Intervention

The AFASIC Language Checklists   LDA. ISBN 1 85503 114 0

Speech and language screening tests for children aged 4–5 and 6–10.

Early Language Skills Checklist   James Boyle & Elizabeth McLellan.
                                           Hodder & Stoughton, ISBN 0 340 663510

Observation-based checklist for children aged 3–5 years with language difficulties.

Activities & Games

The following publications contain a wealth of ideas for developing children's speech and language.

Activities for Speaking & Listening Part 1: Ages 3 to 7
                                           AFASIC. ISBN 0951249940

Activities for Speaking & Listening Part 2: Ages 7 to 11
                                           AFASIC. ISBN 0951249991

Working With Children's Language   Jackie Cooke & Diana Williams.
                                           Winslow Press. ISBN 0863880258

The Language GAP   Sue Gowers & Libby Sisson.
A basic language programme, which looks at auditory memory, categorisation, verbal absurdities, etc.

AMS Educational.   Tel. 0800 917 3201

Teaching Talking: Teaching Resources Handbook.
                                           Ann Locke & Maggie Beech.
                                           NFER-Nelson. ISBN 4037074

Early Language Skills Checklist (as above). Useful section on planning and implementing a language programme, also includes suggestions for activities.

Early Communication Skills   C. Lynch & J. Kidd.
                                          Winslow. ISBN 0863882234

Phonology

Total Phonology: Assessment & Intervention Manual
                                           L. Abba, S. Ayub & V. Selwyn-Barnett.
                                           Winslow. ISBN 0863882048

Children's Phonology Sourcebook   L. Flynn & G. Lancaster.
                                           Winslow. ISBN 086388156 4

Working with Children's Phonology   G. Lancaster & L. Pope.
                                           Winslow. ISBN 086388069X

Social Communication

Semantic-Pragmatic Language Disorder
C. Firth & K. Venkatesh.
Winslow. ISBN 086388203X

Social Skills Stories/More Social Skills Stories
A. Johnson & J. Susnik.
Don Johnston Special Needs.
Tel. 01925 256500

Social Use of Language Programme (SULP)
Wendy Rinaldi.
NFER-Nelson. ISBN 0-7087-0556-1

Talkabout: A Social Communication Skills Package
Alex Kelly.
Winslow. ISBN 0863881467

Don't Take It So Literally: Activities for Teaching Idioms
D. Legler. ECL Publications.

Visual Cues

The Picture Exchange Communication System (PECS)
L. Frost & A. Bondy.
Pyramid Educational Consultants UK Ltd.
Tel. 01273 728888 www.pecs-uk.com

The Picture Communication Symbols Books (PCS)
Roxanna Johnson.
Don Johnston Special Needs.
Tel. 01925 256503

Software

Boardmaker: A Graphics Database Containing 3,000+ Picture Communication Symbols
(see above)
Don Johnston Special Needs.
Tel. 01925 256500

Clicker 4: pictures and words in grids to help sequencing, language and writing skills.
Crick Software.
Tel. 01604 671691 www.cricksoft.com

Picture Sentence Key: Language Structuring Software for Children with Autism and Other Language Disorders.
Don Johnston Special Needs.
Tel. 01925 256500

References

Circle Time
M. Curry & C. Bromfield.
NASEN. ISBN 090673097X

Speech & Language Difficulties
B. Daines, P. Fleming & C. Miller.
NASEN. ISBN 0906730872

Listening & Speaking for All   Sylvia Edwards.
David Fulton Publishers (1999).
ISBN 1 85346 603 4

Pinpointing Language   Anne Keating.
'Special!' Autumn 1998.

IEPs: Speech & Language   J. Tod & M. Blamires.
David Fulton Publishers (1998).
ISBN 1 85346 522 4

Spoken Language Difficulties   Lynn Stuart, Felicity Wright,
Sue Grigor & Alison Howey.
David Fulton Publishers (2002).
ISBN 1 85346 855 X

Helping Language Development   Cooper, Moodley & Reynell (1978).
St Martin's Press.
ISBN 0 31236 757 0

Children's Reading Problems   Bradley & Bryant (1985).
ISBN 0 631 13683 5

Phonemic Analysis and Synthesis As Word Attack Skills
Fox & Routh (1976).

Onset and Rimes as Units of Spoken Syllables
Treiman (1985).
Journal of Experimental Child Psychology **39**

Human Cognitive Neuropsychology   Ellis & Young (1988).
Erlbaum.

National Literacy Strategy   Department for Education and
Employment (1998).

Speaking, Listening, Learning: Working with Children in KS1 & 2
Qualifications and Curriculum
Authority (2003).

Acknowledgements

Information, advice and support provided by:

SENSS Admin staff – Kingston Upon Hull

Hull and East Riding Speech and Language Therapy Support Service.

Good listening rules

✓ good looking

✓ good sitting

✓ good thinking